Bridges to the Soul

A Journey of Love and Connection."

By

Dr Jason Trevor

Table of Contents

INTRODUCTION

This book, "Bridges to the Soul: Journey of Love and Connection," takes us on a poignant journey through how love and connection impact our lives. We will travel together through both actual and metaphorical bridges within the pages of this book as we learn about the transformational, healing, and unifying power of love.

The idea that love is more than an emotion and may lead us to better understand ourselves and other people lies at the center of our investigation. Our road to understanding the core of who we are and the bonds that bind us to people around us is connection— the bridge we construct and cross on this journey.

This book provides ideas, anecdotes, and thoughts to help you navigate the process of understanding love, whether your goals are to comprehend the role of love in your life or to restore broken relationships. Come along with us as we explore the pathways that lead to love, comprehension, and deep connection as we negotiate the intricacies of the heart and soul—greetings on your voyage.

Dr Jason Trevor

Chapter 1

Foundations of the Bridge

Every time something happens, there's usually a spark at first—a small but profound realization that we're all on a journey to connect—for those infrequent instances when our spirits seem to say, "Ah, there you are. I had been trying to find you." This chapter provides the framework for our journey: a search for the various relationships we make and the love we pursue throughout our lives, not simply for romantic love.

Consider love to be the oldest bridge in the world. It is ingrained in our being and has been there for so long that we occasionally cross it without realizing it. It's in the calming lullaby a mother gives her infant, the consoling stillness between long-time friends, and the comprise-shrilling excitement of forming a new bond. The architecture of our inner existence is made up of these links, these bridges.

However, the materials we use to construct these bridges are particular to each of us, molded by our individual experiences—successes and disappointments. The paradox of love and connection is that although they are universal goals, there are countless ways in which we might experience and express them. You are invited to consider your foundations in this chapter—the beliefs and experiences that have shaped how you view love and relationships.

We discover the beauty of vulnerability as we explore the nature of these feelings. Opening up to someone else means letting them see us for who we are—warts and all. It's terrifying and thrilling simultaneously because we find a genuine connection at that moment of transparency.

We'll examine how empathy and communication serve as the cornerstones of this bridge we're creating through stories and reflections.The foundation of our relationships is made up of sharing and listening, as well as understanding and being understood.

As we wrap up this chapter, consider the bridges you have established in your life. Each one bears witness to the human ability for love and connection, regardless of whether it is strong or in need of repair. Beyond merely comprehending these forces, this trip we are doing together is about honoring and fostering them in our lives.

So, shall we start now? Keeping in mind that every step we take brings us closer to the core of what it is to love and be loved, let's examine the foundations of our bridges with open hearts and minds.

Dr Jason Trevor

Chapter 2

Building the Bridge

Think of building a bridge as an art form, where each of us is an artist with our palette of emotions, experiences, and hopes. The first stroke of the brush is always a gesture of openness, an invitation for others to step into our world. It's about sharing our true selves, our dreams, fears, and joys, and in doing so, we create a space for genuine connection.

The various ways we can build these bridges are outlined in this chapter. It all begins with the small but essential act of listening; hearing is not the same as comprehending the feelings and sensations conveyed via words. Trust and empathy are the cornerstones of any meaningful relationship, and listening builds them.

However, it can be challenging to create bridges. It necessitates navigating the abyss of misunderstandings and misinterpretation and knowing how to respectfully and honestly communicate our needs and desires. Here, we explore the craft of communication and provide tips on ensuring our words create connections rather than divides.

Our bridges are reminding us of the strength of vulnerability as they start to take shape. It's the bravery to be seen, to show up, and to see other people. Deep, meaningful connections are made possible by vulnerability, which is the cornerstone of the bridge and the element that holds everything else in place.

Throughout this chapter, we'll tell tales of bridges established between people of all ages, backgrounds, and walks of life in unexpected locations, reminding us of the strength of vulnerability as they action and the unique ways it might materialize if we're willing to explore new avenues.

We'd ask you to consider the connections you're making. Recall that every attempt at communication, every instance of openness and understanding, is a step towards creating a world in which love and connection can cover the breadth of the human experience.

With our tools in hand and prepared to construct bridges that will endure the test of time, space, and change, let's continue on our adventure. We weave a web of relationships that improves our and those around us when we work together.

An older woman named Edith lived in a busy urban neighborhood where the streets were a patchwork of cultures, and the air buzzed with the energy of many lives colliding. Her days were peaceful in contrast to the lively world outside her window. Continued no relatives nearby and herself bereaved, she took comfort in her books and the recollections of a life well spent.

Alex moved into the same flat building a few doors down. He was a young immigrant with big hopes and a strong will to start over in this strange country. Despite the many obstacles, including linguistic and cultural differences, Alex's spirit did not falter.

One frigid evening, Edith was outside the building fumbling with her groceries when their paths unexpectedly collided. After a tiring day at work, Alex jumped at the chance to help. This small deed of kindness was the first stone thrown on the bridge to span their two worlds.

The days stretched into weeks, and Edith and Alex began to see each other more often. A nod became a greeting, a hello became small talk, and small talk developed into deep discussions. With her extensive knowledge and experience, Edith told stories about a world Alex had only ever read about in books. In return, Alex told stories about his country, culture, and aspirations for the future.

Their friendship took an unexpected turn for the better. They began dining together, with Edith showing Alex how to prepare classic recipes from her childhood and Alex introducing Edith to the tastes of his native country. These dinners turned into a spiritual place for them to communicate, laugh, and gain knowledge from one another.

Despite decades separating them and vastly different upbringings, this odd pair established a deep bond. They had filled a gap they hadn't known existed by becoming each other's families. Their relationship proved that relationships may be made despite differences in age, culture, and life experiences in the most unlikely settings.

The tale of Edith and Alex proves the value of candor, generosity, and the need for connection candor in every human being. It serves as a reminder that despite the distance we've traveled or the routes we've crossed, understanding and love are always accessible and waiting to be developed when we approach them with open minds and hearts.

Their narrative is a ray of hope, showing how accepting the range of human experience can result in the most fulfilling and surprising relationships, improving our lives in ways we never would have imagined.

Dr Jason Trevor

Chapter 3

Crossing the Bridge

Reaching the connecting bridge is like setting off on a voyage that has sun and storms, but it is during this journey that love indeed reveals its transformative power. This chapter walks us through the core of these life-changing experiences, illuminating them with anecdotes that perfectly depict the power of love to transform lives, mend hurts, and unexpectedly bring people closer.

Imagine a bridge that crosses a vast canyon, with distinct views from either side. Silence was on one side, shared laughter was on the other; seclusion was on one side, friendship was on the other. Crossing this bridge takes courage and beauty, but it also represents a dedication to understanding and unity.

Sarah yearns for more meaningful interactions after years of putting her profession ahead of her relationships. She chooses to cross the bridge, which enables her to get in touch with long-lost relatives and friends and reintegrate into the community of mutual support and shared experiences. Every stride she takes across the bridge symbolizes a step closer to living a more fulfilled and connected life on her path to rediscovery.

Next is the tale of Daniel and Miguel, two neighbors with minor in common but a wall they shared. Through a sequence of exchanged

Difficulties progress from courteous nods to deep talks before finally crossing a bridge of respect and comprehension. Their changing relationship exemplifies how hardship may act as a spark for friendship, converting strangers into allies and friends into allies again.

Think back to the neighborhood project that united individuals with various backgrounds to establish a communal garden. This connection bridge grew from shared soil, where hands that had previously worked independently combined to nourish life involved in unity's power in a simply lovely setting, to a representation of love and teamwork, teaching all those concerned about the power of unity.

Think about the story of Emma, who connects with her grandfather Arthur by reaching over the generational gap. They rebuild their relationship by telling one another stories and spending quiet moments together, regaining love and friendship. Emma discovers her heritage, and Arthur, nearing the end of his life, finds fresh happiness; their relationship blossoms in the common area where the past and present meet.

Every narrative in this chapter, from Sarah's renewed friendships to the group bonds forged in a garden, acts as a lighthouse, pointing the way through the difficulties and rewards of bridging the gap between love and connection. These stories serve as a helpful reminder that, despite the difficulty of reaching out, the process of doing so is complete with learning and personal growth.

We are encouraged to consider the bridges in our own lives that still need to be crossed as we wrap up this chapter. There are numerous ways to connect with people; every step we take towards

comprehension, recovery, and the deep satisfaction of

genuine connections with people is a step closer. Let us welcome

the journey with open hearts, for love's enduring power and the

prospect of fresh starts await us on the other side of each bridge.

Chapter 4

Repairing Broken Bridges

We frequently come across times during the path of love and connection when the bridges we've laboriously constructed seem to waver or even fall apart. Disagreements, misunderstandings, and time can all lead to insurmountable gaps. However, rebuilding these damaged bridges involves more than just patching relationships; it entails rediscovering the resiliency and strength underpinnings.

This chapter explores the art and heart of reconciliation, highlighting how acting to mend a broken relationship is a significant act of bravery and love. It's about moving forward with empathy and a genuine will to understand, even in the face of our own and other people's shortcomings.

To mend shattered bridges, we must face our shadows, including our pride, anxieties, and hesitations. It challenges us to pay attention—to the other side of the tale, to the feelings and experiences that molded how things are today. This technique aims to comprehend the complexity of human connections rather than place blame.

Our most helpful instrument, therefore, becomes communication. We can find reconciliation and the actions required to reestablish affection and trust by having an open, sincere, and caring conversation. Patience and persistence are your allies in this delicate dance of give and take.

Along the way, forgiveness is essential. The bridge enables us to move from hurt and wrath towards recovery and serenity. To forgive is to be freed from past wrongs' grip on our present and future, not to condone them. It's a gift we give ourselves and each other, a first step in mending the spiritual and emotional bonds that tie us.

The change that occurs when damaged bridges are repaired makes them so beautiful. Relationships that have survived and become more robust due to conflict are examples of the enduring power of love and connection. They serve as a reminder that no bridge is damaging and that every attempt to patch a divide is a step towards a more meaningful and profound connection.

We're left feeling hopeful and reaffirmed in our confidence that our relationships have the capacity to heal and grow as we close this chapter. The process of rebuilding damaged bridges is evidence of the human spirit's forgiving, loving, and evolving nature, with the understanding that although bridges may collapse, we can fix them.

Dr Jason Trevor

Chapter 5

Infinite Bridges

We discover that the bridges we construct are limitless and not just temporary buildings as we continue our trip toward the center of connection. They reach into the future and impact lives in ways we can hardly fathom, going beyond the present moment. This chapter affirms that our connections can transcend time and space and leave a lasting legacy beyond our lives. It does this by celebrating the eternal legacy of love and connection.

We are prompted to consider the nature of our relationships and the essence of our interactions by the idea of limitless bridges. It emphasises how much our words, deeds, and capacity for love have an influence. Every nice deed, every understanding moment, and every supportive gesture adds up to form a brick in the ever-growing bridge that binds us to people in the present and the future.

This enduring quality of connection modifies generations, changes lives, and shapes communities. It's understanding that even something as basic as a tale told, a lesson imparted, or an act of kindness may have a lasting impact that uplifts and inspires people long after we have moved on. It shows that our power transcends the confines of our physical existence.

Accepting the concept of infinite bridges pushes us to take greater intentionality in our lives and relationships. It inspires us to think about the legacy we want to leave behind and how our deeds today might affect people we may never meet. It appeals to action to help create a society based on compassion, empathy, and understanding.

This chapter also serves as a reminder that love—in all its manifestations—is the most potent force for good in our lives and the wider world. Love is the best material for building bridges; it can unite people across gaps, mend broken hearts, and endure a lifetime and beyond.

The consoling and empowering idea that the love we offer and the connections we foster have the capacity to leave a lasting legacy is what we take with us as we finish this chapter. It serves as a reminder that, within the vast fabric of life, each of us has the potential to weave a web of unending bridges made possible by the enduring force of love and the unwavering spirit of human connection.

Dr Jason Trevor

Chapter 6

Bridges to the Soul

The most significant bridges—bridges to the soul—are made in a sacred place at the center of our journey, between the chapters of connection and the infinite. This chapter explores how love, in its purest form, acts as a bridge to our innermost selves, promoting spiritual development and personal transformation. It also explores the essence of these connections.

Recognising our shared humanity and getting a glimpse of another person's experience, which mirrors our weaknesses, skills, and goals, is fundamental to recognizing every meaningful relationship. It is not just words or deeds that build these bridges to the spirit; it is also the shared grin, the silent understanding, and the consoling presence that says, "I see you, I understand you, and you are not alone."

Building a bridge to another person's soul is a profoundly empathic journey that requires us to leave our world and enter that of the other. We discover the transformational power of connection in this holy exchange—not merely as a means of support but also as a method of mutual growth and enlightenment.

This chapter emphasizes the value of being fully there and with someone at all times—not just during happy times but also throughout difficult and depressing ones. During these times, the combined light of our group spirit strengthens the bridges to the soul. It serves as a reminder that, in the end, the most significant relationships are those that touch the soul, reawaken something buried deep within us, and inspire us to reach our full potential.

Furthermore, the path to meaningful connection is a path to personal growth. We see our potential, our growth areas, and the beauty of our journeys when we look at ourselves in the reflection of others. These links remind us of the interconnection of all life and our inherent worth by serving as mirrors, compass points, and anchors.

We are encouraged to consider the bridges we have made and those we still need to build as we wrap up this chapter. It's an appeal to build relationships beyond appearances, looking for and caring for those unique and exquisite bridges to the spirit that profoundly improve our lives. With hearts wide open, let us proceed, eager to discover the depth of connection that arises when two souls come into contact, comprehend, and support one another—leaving a legacy of love and development that goes beyond the limitations of our temporary existence on Earth.

Dr Jason Trevor

Chapter 7

The Echoes of Love and Connection

As our journey through the domains of love and connection ends, we find ourselves on the brink of an endless vista, where the ripples of our relationships extend into eternity and beyond the confines of time and space. This chapter affirms the importance of love in forming the universe's fabric beyond our direct line of sight by going deeper into the reflection of love's enduring influence and the tremendous legacy left by our connections.

Love is a phenomenon that endures beyond the confines of our bodily existence. Once it is in motion, this force never stops inspiring and influencing people, even after the events that gave rise to it have passed. The idea that our deeds of kindness and love have a lasting impression on humanity and are remembered by those impacted by our lives is reaffirmed in this chapter.

We learn that the breadth and quality of our relationships, rather than our outward achievements or plaudits, will determine our legacy. It's etched in the lives we've impacted, the hearts we've touched, and the love we've experienced together. Our genuine gift to the world is this intangible inheritance, which demonstrates the ability of human connection to go beyond the confines of our earthly existence.

The stories passed down through the years, the lessons of empathy and compassion that parents teach their children, and the deeds of kindness that encourage others to do the same all echo love and connection. With the best intentions and the essence of our spirits, these echoes create a bridge connecting the past and the future.

We are inspired to live with purpose and love without boundaries as we consider the enduring power of love and the legacy of our relationships. Making decisions that promote love, understanding, and togetherness is made more accessible when we are aware of the impact of our actions today on the world of tomorrow. It is an exhortation to take a constructive part in humanity's continuing story and appeal to design a future based on love and connection.

As we end this chapter and possibly our trip through this book, we are reminded of the human heart's limitless ability for love, connection, and the creation of enduring legacies. Accepting this insight, let's go forth, knowing that our lives and love have significance that extends well beyond our immediate vision, reverberating through the ages and affecting souls we may never meet but will always affect.

This contemplation of the eternal quality of love and the legacy of our relationships challenges us to see our lives as essential strands in the enormous fabric of human existence, woven together by the transformative and timeless power of love rather than as isolated journeys.

Dr Jason Trevor

Conclusion

The Journey Home

We take a moment to consider our shared trip as we near the end of our investigation into the deep domains of love and connection. We have traveled the emotional landscapes via the pages of this book, finding the links that bind us to the most profound aspects of ourselves and each other. This trip has been one of self-discovery and validation, bringing to light the reality that love—in all of its manifestations—is the cornerstone around which our lives and the planet are constructed.

Love can elevate the commonplace to the sublime, transforming small deeds of kindness into the cornerstones of enduring relationships. We've admired the human spirit's tenacity in the face of difficulties and transformations, and we've seen firsthand the power of empathy, understanding, and vulnerability in creating connections that cut beyond boundaries.

Let's take the knowledge and understanding we have obtained with us as we proceed from this point on. Recall that each encounter presents a chance to construct a fresh bridge, extend our hand beyond the gap of miscommunication and anxiety, and illuminate another person's soul with the essence of our humanity. The bridges we construct are the fundamental structure of a more sympathetic and interconnected world; they are more than just conduits for love.

This book serves as an invitation to let love and connection in all of its manifestations into your heart. It inspires you to treasure the relationships that feed your soul and make the brave and curious journey of seeking new ones through an expansive and breathtaking terrain. Love and connection are a never-ending adventure that presents countless chances for growth, joy, and discovery.

Let this not be a farewell as we part ways, but rather a gentle prod to embark on your journeys of love and connection. Recall that the bridges you have already crossed and those you still need to construct are the monuments on your trip, bringing you one step closer to your actual self and the heart that beats for all people.

This path of love and connection is ultimately a voyage home, a return to the knowledge that the invisible strands of love and our shared humanity bind us all together. Thus, let us go on our journey with hearts wide open, creating new connections, valuing the relationships that enrich our lives, and interlacing the golden threads of love into the intricate fabric of our everyday lives.

Thank you for sharing this journey with me. May your path be illuminated by love, and may your bridges be many and magnificent, leading you ever closer to the heart of what it means to be truly connected, truly alive.

www.ingramcontent.com/pod-product-compliance
Lightning Source LLC
Chambersburg PA
CBHW070750260726
48660CB00007B/3048